How to Grow Mushrooms at Home

Guide to Indoor Mushroom Farming for Health and Profit

Includes fungiculture information, health and medicinal benefits, editable mushrooms, selling mushrooms, mushroom kits, and composting

By Randall Frank

How to Grow Mushrooms at Home

Guide to Indoor Mushroom Farming for Health and Profit

Author: Randall Frank

Published by: Homesteading Publishers, homesteadingpublishers.com

ISBN: 978-1-927870-22-8

Dedication

I would like to thank my immediate family for allowing me the freedom to experiment with trying to grow edible mushrooms over the years. It took me a while to find success, and when I did, I tried to get my father into this lucrative hobby. This book is dedicated to his memory. I love you, Dad.

Disclaimer

This book is designed to provide information on indoor mushroom growing only. This information is provided and sold with the knowledge that the publisher and author do not offer any legal, health, or other professional advice. In the case of a need for any such expertise consult with the appropriate professional. This book does not contain all information available on the subject. This book has not been created to be specific to any individual's or organizations' situation or needs. Every effort has been made to make this book as accurate as possible. However, there may be typographical and or content errors. Therefore, this book should serve only as a general guide and not as the ultimate source of subject information. This book contains information that might be dated and is intended only to educate and entertain. The author and publisher shall have no liability or responsibility to any person or entity regarding any loss or damage incurred, or alleged to have incurred, directly or indirectly, by the information contained in this book. You hereby agree to be bound by this disclaimer or you may return this book within the guarantee time period for a full refund.

Foreword

Learn about how you can be a part of 'fungiculture' and grow mushrooms at home for health and profit.

This book explains how mushrooms grow, how to grow mushrooms, what mushrooms to grow, and the amazing health benefits of eating certain types of mushrooms.

You will discover mushrooms are easy to grow and many have protein, B vitamins, minerals and some tout medicinal properties such as boosting the immune system, lowering cholesterol, and having a positive effect on certain cancers. In addition there are tips, methods, and insider techniques for growing mushrooms and marketing them.

Acknowledgements

When I returned to mushroom cultivation after some time away, there were many bloggers that inspired me with their creative shiitake mushroom growing. I would consider it "art" in some form, and I attempted to recreate it. My love of the hobby just grew from there. There are too many people to thank, and I don't want to risk leaving anyone out, so I will just say the bloggers and online forum contributors deserve most of the credit for this book being written. Without them, I wouldn't have shared as much knowledge to help get started producing mushrooms in a financially profitable manner while being environmentally sustainable.

Table of Contents

1. Introduction to Mushrooms

"Nature alone is antique, and the oldest art a mushroom."
--Thomas Carlyle

Mushrooms are not a fruit or vegetable or even a plant. They are fruiting bodies of fungus or fungi (pronounced, fun gee or fun guy.)

'Fungiculture' is the practice of producing food, medicine, and further products by cultivating mushrooms and additional fungi. Americans consume about 900 million pounds of mushrooms a year and most of those are the white button mushroom and, in the same family, the Cremini and Portobello mushrooms.

You can practice 'fungiculture' or grow mushrooms for health and profit. They are fairly easy to grow and many have protein, B vitamins, minerals and some tout medicinal properties such as boosting the immune system, lowering cholesterol, and having a positive effect on breast cancer in women and prostate cancer in men.

There might be as many as 140,000 species of mushrooms. Only about ten per cent or 14,000 of them have been identified. Out of all those different kinds of mushrooms, only about 250 species are edible. Currently approximately

100 species of mushrooms are being researched for medicinal benefits.

The largest commercial producer of mushrooms in the world is China and then the United States where almost three fourths of U.S. mushrooms are grown on the east coast.

Mushrooms are a Super Food

There is ample evidence supporting mushrooms as a "super food" packed with potent nutrition. Health conscious consumers prefer organically grown mushrooms to steer clear of any harmful contaminants and health experts recommend exclusively eating organically grown mushrooms. Mushrooms easily absorb elements from their growth environment, such as soil, air and water in concentrated quantities.

Mushrooms are rich with beneficial nutrition and low in fat, calories and cholesterol. There are 2 grams of protein, a healthy dose of potassium and three important B vitamins in an average serving. Mushrooms also contain selenium found in meats. That makes mushrooms an adequate selenium source for vegetarians.

Certain mushrooms are a diet staple of some people, while other species are more of a delicacy. The mounting knowledge of their health benefits has contributed to their growing popularity and demand.

People look for organically grown mushrooms due to the fact that mushrooms are porous and absorb good and bad elements from the air, water, and substrate where they are grown. They concentrate any heavy metals and pollutants present.

Ancient Chinese medicine discovered the health benefits of mushrooms thousands of years ago including their aid in boosting immunity. The human make up is closely related to fungi as we share the equivalent pathogens, or bacteria and viruses. The antibiotics developed by fungi to protect themselves against bacteria are also effective for us. Some examples include penicillin, streptomycin, and tetracycline.

Numerous studies have shown varied health benefits of a variety of mushrooms. One such study showed that regular mushroom consumption was directly related to better nutrition. Eating dried white button mushroom extract is the same as taking vitamin D2 or D3 supplements. This mushroom also contains protein, enzymes, B vitamins, and vitamin D2.

Mushrooms are low calorie and great sources of antioxidants, including polyphenols and selenium, as well as antioxidants unique to mushrooms, such as ergothioneine.

Another study found that substituting red meat with white button mushrooms can assist in losing weight.

In addition to the culinary uses of mushrooms people take mushroom supplements. There are basically two types of mushroom supplements.

Mushroom Concentrates and Extracts

In order to get these extracts, the mushroom mycelia or fruit body is placed in boiling water for some time to remove the long chain polysaccharides. What you are left with is a concentrated form of glycol-nutrients or complex sugars. These are where the mushroom's health benefits are thought to be.

Raw or Whole Food Mushrooms

These supplements are in the form of a powdered pill and generally taken by people striving to maintain optimal health.

Medicinal Benefits

Research supports the many medicinal benefits of a variety of mushrooms.

For example, [1]Cordyceps, also called caterpillar fungus or Tochukasu, has a history of use in medicine by the Chinese and Tibetans dating far back. Athletes benefit from an increase in ATP production, strength and endurance. This mushroom also has anti-aging effects, and can help enhance female fertility by improving the in vitro success rate (IVF).

This fungi also has shown to have positive possibilities for hypoglycemic and antidepressant effects, increasing blood flow, normalizing cholesterol levels, and has been implemented in treatment for Hepatitis B.

More recent research shows promise for prevention and treatment of immune disorders, cancer and as a potent anti-inflammatory agent for asthma, rheumatoid arthritis, renal failure, and stroke damage.

World Mushroom Production

World mushroom production has been greatly increasing. In 1965, about 350,000 metric tons were produced.[2] By 1997, this increased to 6,160,800 metric tons or by over 1700 per

---

[1] http://articles.mercola.com/sites/articles/archive/2013/05/13/mushroom-benefits.aspx

[2] http://pubs.cas.psu.edu/freepubs/pdfs/ul207.pdf

cent. During 2010-2011, the U.S. alone produced 862 million pounds of mushrooms valued at $1.02 billion.[3]

The button mushroom which 30 years ago accounted for 70 per cent of all mushroom production, now represents less than 30 per cent of mushrooms produced. Estimates are that oyster mushrooms now account for close to 20 per cent of total world production. Consumer demand has driven the growth and market prices for this mushroom which requires less technology and risk for cultivation, essentially making this a profitable crop for growers.

---

[3] http://www.agmrc.org/commodities__products/specialty_crops/mushrooms/

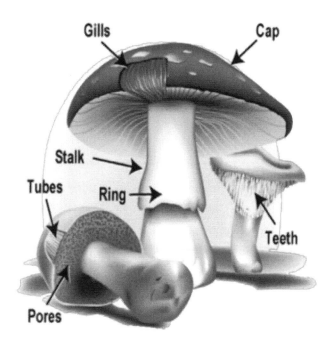

How Mushrooms Grow

Mushrooms do not need any light to grow. Only green plants need light for photosynthesis. Air circulation is necessary to grow mushrooms and help maintain humidity and temperature. Environmental requirements for most mushrooms are achievable at home.

Mushrooms do not have seed and are grown from spores that are not visible to the human eye without magnification. Plant seeds contain chlorophyll which helps them germinate. Mushrooms, however, do not contain chlorophyll and rely on external materials such as wood, sawdust, grain, wooden plugs, straw, or liquid for sustenance. This process is known as reverse photosynthesis. Mushrooms take in carbon and consume oxygen. Plants, on the other hand, consume carbon dioxide and produce carbon and oxygen.

Mushrooms start as spores that are released from the gills or pores beneath the cap similar to dust. When mushrooms reproduce, they multiply by putting out millions of spores. Spores settling in fitting environments develop into mycelium, which is a network of damp fibers. These fibers utilize powerful enzymes to enter their substrate such as straw, wood or other organic material. The mycelium gets nourishment from digesting the wood. The mycelium develops when mushrooms are ready to reproduce. The spores are created in the gills and then released to initiate new mycelia elsewhere.

A mix of the spores and nutrients is known as "spawn". The spawn supports the growth of the roots. The mushrooms have small, white, threadlike roots, called "mycelium". These roots begin growing before the actual mushroom.

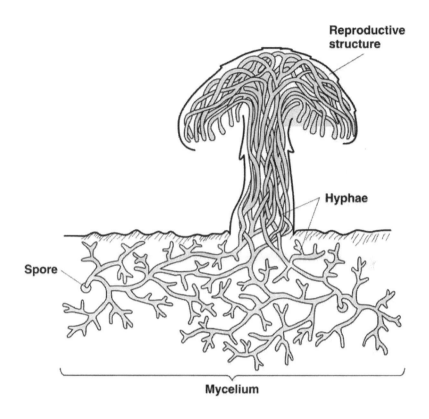

Image Source: http://www.chesterfield.k12.sc.us/

Most mushrooms grown indoors are primary decomposers. This type of mushroom can break down wood chips or logs to eat. The Agaricus genus family members are secondary decomposers. These mushrooms need other fungi or bacteria to break down wood into compost before they can utilize this for food. The secondary decomposers require a more complicated

21

cultivation process. Fungi direct the natural decomposition cycles and are critical to biological systems and humans.

Fungi Life Cycle

When cultivating edible mushrooms, spores are not used because they are too small and mushroom spores take considerable time to germinate.

Pre-grown mycelium of the mushroom is inoculated on a sterile substrate and this is known as spawn. Spawn placed in sterilized substrate give the cultivated mushroom a head start above other fungi. The mycelium then colonizes the substrate feeding on the nutrients. This period is known as the spawn run where mycelium then begins fruiting. Factors that can induce fruiting include a changing temperature, high humidity, loss of or deficiency of a nutrient, a high CO_2 concentration in the air, or light, depending on the type of mushroom. Most of these factors that stimulate fruiting have a harmful consequence on the mycelium. So when cultivating changes intended to induce fruiting, this should only be done if the mycelium growth has gone through the substrate.

The mycelium reproduces when the nutrients have been all used or the environment changes.

Toxic Mushrooms

While only about 100 mushroom species are toxic, as many as 6,000 Americans eat these every year and some result in death caused by amatoxins. Because these are mushrooms growing in the wild, unfortunately the majority of those victims are small children.

If you forage for wild mushrooms, make certain you supervise children and know how to identify edible species from toxic mushrooms.

If you suspect that someone has eaten a poisonous mushroom, get the person to a hospital immediately. Amanitin poisoning has no known anecdote, so medical attention is required to remove toxins.

2. Introduction to Growing Mushrooms Indoors

In a dry or winter climate, growing mushrooms indoors is often the only option. Mushrooms can be grown indoors year-round. Although growing indoors can require more work, it produces the best mushrooms and yields.

If you are seeking extra or full time income, an alternative way to garden during the off season, or specific nutritional or medicinal benefits, growing mushrooms indoors might be your answer.

Growing mushrooms on a small scale is not difficult once you are armed with the knowledge of how mushrooms grow and their needs.

Mushrooms are simple organisms that grow in the dark with some humidity. Mushrooms can be grown indoors in any climate and in any season and nearly anywhere with the right conditions, including basements and crawl spaces, as well as other other smaller spaces like apartments. These funguses are one of only a few plants that grow without chlorophyll. They get all their nutrition from the material or substrate they grow in or on. A substrate can be straw or wood chips.

You need a growing room where you can control the temperature. Your growing room should maintain a temperature of 78 degrees Fahrenheit (25 degrees Celsius). You also need to be able to control the humidity and the light.

Cleanliness is also critical to healthy mushroom growth, as there are numerous possible contaminates that can harm or ruin mushrooms. Pasteurizing the substrate or straw is a great start for eliminating possible contaminates. All growing area surfaces and tools should be cleaned with a 10% bleach solution before adding the substrate. Wash your hands every time and thoroughly before you handle your spawn, substrate, or tools.

There are supplements that can be added during the growing process to enhance flavor and increase yields, including soy, cottonseed and alfalfa meal.

Mushroom Kits

Image Source: http://sustainability.sbcc.edu

Mushroom kits are available with ready-to-inoculate spawn. These kits come with spores and all the supplies needed to get started growing. The simplest mushroom growing kits include a bag of sawdust or straw that has been inoculated with spawn.

Kits include full instructions and some have plastic tents for controlling humidity. Basically, you find a location that is room temperature and away from any direct sunlight for your setup and substrate. Then you spray mist several times a day for humidity.

The next chapter details the different culinary mushroom types that are popular for home growers that include cremini, oysters, shiitake, wine caps and portabellas, yet there are more.

Making Money Growing Mushrooms

When you learn the art of growing mushrooms, you might decide to grow for profit. Gourmet mushrooms are a valuable crop, though you should have your market in place. Where you can sell will depend on the quantity and types of mushrooms you grow, as well as your location. As consumer demand has increased as awareness of the health benefits has spread. The market for mushrooms is better than ever and medicinal mushroom research is aiding the demand for more species.

Mushroom growing can be rewarding and profitable. The barrier to entry is more knowledge than cost as expensive equipment is not needed. However, there is a learning curve. Timing can be somewhat tricky, and certain species entail intense management.

Gourmet mushrooms are enjoying a growing popularity. This increasing demand has created profitable opportunities even for small indoor farming with the exotic mushrooms, such as oyster and Shiitake mushrooms.

Oyster mushrooms are a gourmet mushroom that is profitable for the home grower due to demand and the low expense barrier to growing. The oyster mushroom grows quickly and a home grower can produce about five crops annually, even in their spare time of as little as a few hours per week.

Due to the fact that oyster mushrooms are so fruitful, even a small space can produce good income. In fact, a growing area of about 100 square feet can produce as much as 2,500 pounds of mushrooms a year! In an area as small as five hundred square feet, about 12,000 pounds of mushrooms can be grown and harvested annually. When retail prices for oyster mushrooms are at about $6 per pound, which they have been, that equates to a gross income of $72,000 annually.

Your chances of success can greatly increase with the knowledge gained from this book as well as a curiosity and passion for fungi.

Selling Mushrooms

Because fresh mushrooms bring the most money and sell the best you want to sell your mushrooms when you harvest them whenever possible. Any mushrooms you do not sell can be frozen or dried to sell later.

Be prepared ahead of time to market your mushrooms. Learn about any farmers' markets that are within a reasonable distance of your location. These markets can draw large crowds, including market and restaurant owners as well as other buyers. These can be great contacts and you could have commitments from buyers for your future crops before you even begin growing.

Restaurants look for unique and local produce; mushrooms are no exception. Make the rounds in your area and meet restaurant owners. Give them free samples and let them know your harvest schedule.

Grocery stores and some health food stores stock mushrooms and many also appreciate local growers. If you can supply them with fresh gourmet mushrooms, you might not need any other customers. You can ask stores if you can set up a free sample table for a day to cater to their customers, also.

The Future of Mushrooms

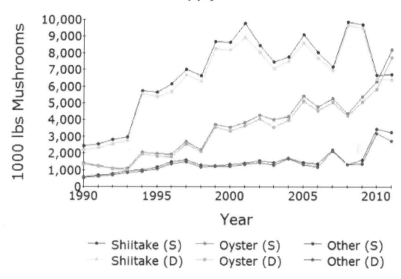

Image Source: http://greennature.com/article424.html

People are becoming educated about the health benefits and culinary characteristics of mushrooms. Demand is increasing. Cultivation technology continues to advance as fueled by the demand. Research is being done to increase the shelf life of mushrooms including packaging technology and storage, as well as improving the mushrooms themselves, which will help to meet the demand.

Research into the medicinal benefits of mushroom also continues and as new advantages are discovered. This will also cause demand to increase. The ease of producing mushrooms on a small scale makes this a perfect income opportunity for many people.

3. Types of Mushrooms

Mushrooms are divided into categories based on how they feed. There are basically four mushroom categories: saprotrophic, mycorrhizal, parasitic, and endophytic.

Saprotrophs: Thrive on Decay

Saprotrophic mushrooms use specific enzymes and acids to help decompose dead tissue from trees, other plants, and sometimes mammals. They do this to break down these substances for their food. Saprotrophs play a vital role in nature's decomposition and food chain.

Saprotroph mushrooms include:

- White Buttons
- Morels
- Reishi
- Shiitake
- Cremini
- Oysters
- Maitake
- Turkey Tail
- Giant Puffball
- Chicken of the Woods (also a parasitic mushroom)
- Enoki or Enokitake
- Shaggy Mane

- Black Trumpet

Mycorrhizae Mushrooms: Partner with Plants

These fungi have a beneficial partnership with plant roots. They grow into the root cells (endomycorrhizal) or wrap around the roots (ectomycorrhizal). The mushrooms give moisture, phosphorous, and nutrients to the trees and get the sugars trees produce. Farmers and gardeners inoculate crops with this fungus to encourage growth.

Most plants in nature have a mycorrhizal partnership with some sort of fungi yet the majority either too hard to cultivate or not edible. Mycorrhizae mushrooms include:

- Caesar's Mushroom
- Chanterelles
- Matsutake
- Porcini
- Truffles

Parasites Mushrooms: Feed on the Weak

Parasitic mushrooms take plant hosts and infect them. This is fatal for the host. Most parasitic fungi do not produce mushrooms until the host is dead or dying. Parasite mushrooms include:

- Honey mushrooms
- Caterpillar Fungus

- Lion's Mane
- Chaga

Endophytes: An Unexplained Symbiosis

The endophytic category partner with plants by invading the host tissue without harming the host and might even benefit them. Many of these species do not produce mushrooms and how they work is still a mystery.

Types of Mushrooms to Grow Indoors

There are many kinds of mushrooms you can grow indoors and each type has particular growing needs. You can order kits for the most commonly grown mushrooms. Choosing what mushroom to grow will depend on your purpose for growing mushrooms (personal use or for income,) resources and space available, geographical location, and so on. The most commonly home grown mushrooms include:

Agaricus: Numerous Agaricus species are grown commercially such as the White Button (Agaricus. Brunnescens,) Portobello (Agaricus Portobello,) also known as "Italian Agaricus" and the Cremini.

Enoki: Enoki or Enokitake mushrooms are also referred to as the winter mushroom and can be found in many grocery stores.

Reishi: Popular in the orient for medicinal properties. Easily grown on conifer and hardwood stumps.

Lion's Mane: Some say this mushroom tastes like lobster.

Maitake: (Hen of the Woods): Grifola frondosa (Polyporus frondosus). This mushroom is in high demand and can grow to be up to 100 pounds.

Nameko: The shiitake mushroom in the most popular in Japan and the Nameko is number two. Nameko (Pholiota nameko) is very simple to grow.

Oyster: There are a variety of cultivated oyster mushrooms species such as: Pearl (Pleurotus ostreatus), Pink (Pleaurotus djamor), Gray (Pleurotus pulmonarius) and more.

Paddy Straw: This mushroom has one of the longest histories and oldest mushrooms in cultivation. This one is easy to grow indoors with a controlled temperature of at least 86-95 Fahrenheit (30-35 degrees Celsius), which is common in greenhouses.

Shiitake: Shiitakes mushrooms are popular for their health benefits. They are easy to grow on straw or hardwoods. There are strains categorized by indoor and outdoor cultivation.

The Agaricus Bisporus Family

The most popular mushrooms for eating are White Buttons, Cremini, and Portobellos. As mentioned, these three mushrooms are all part of the same family known as "Agaricus bisporus." This Latin name Agaricus meaning "gilled mushroom" and bisporus means the spore-producing structures on the gills have two (bi)"rather than four.

The white button is the common mushroom sold in grocery stores and is also known as the table mushroom, common mushroom, champignon de Paris, or the white mushroom. The button mushroom is a saprotroph, defined as feeding on dead or dying organic material.

The cremini mushroom is a brown strain of the white button and is also known as the Italian mushroom, brown mushroom, baby Portobello, or baby bella.

The portobello mushroom is a cremini that has been permitted to grow to maturity and is also known as the portobello, portabella, or cappellone mushroom.

Cremini

Cremini: Agaricus bisporus

Cremini mushrooms, also known as crimini mushrooms, have a strong resemblance to the white button, only the Cremini have a brown cap. Cremini mushrooms are the world's most frequently eaten mushroom. This mushroom is also known as the "button" mushroom. There are a variety of strains (or "isolates") of Agaricus bisporus.

Harvesting these mushrooms in different stages produces a variety of cultivated names. White buttons are harvested early in growth or at an intermediate stage. Cremini are also called baby bellas, baby portobellos, and portobellini or brown mushrooms. Portobellos are older cremini. When cremini mushrooms are permitted to reach full maturity before harvesting they are referred to as Portobello mushrooms.

Wild Cremini have more flavor, firmer texture and a darker brown color than the white button mushrooms commonly found in grocery stores.

Button mushrooms have been present in nature since the beginning of man. The Egyptians believed these mushrooms could give immortality and in Rome they were referred to as "food for the gods." Other culture also thought mushrooms possessed super powers.

Health and Medicinal Benefits

Although cremini mushrooms have nutritional benefits, they do not the medicinal popularity of their cousins -reishi and or maitake. Research has shown the Cremini holds aromatase, an enzyme that aids estrogen production which can help reduce the risk of breast cancer.

Cremini mushrooms are known to contain:

- Vitamin D
- Potassium
- B Vitamins
- Helpful antioxidants like selenium

- Fiber
- Linoleic acid

Immune System Support

Our immune systems are benefited by cremini mushrooms by actually altering how white blood cells operate. In certain studies, the substances in the mushrooms prevent the activity of some white blood cells and activate others.

One key nutrient for a healthy immune system is vitamin D1, which is found in cremini mushrooms.

Anti-Inflammatory Benefits

Chronic inflammation is related to type II diabetes, cardiovascular disease, and some cancers. Fresh mushrooms and extracts as supplements have been proven to reduce and prevent inflammation. Cremini mushrooms have certain inflammatory blocking molecules that work better than shiitake and maitake mushrooms in certain cases.

Antioxidant Benefits

Cremini mushrooms have a nutrient composition that provides antioxidant support and have a positive effect on oxidative metabolism. Their nutrients include the minerals selenium, zinc and manganese which are all vital for antioxidant enzymes.

Cardiovascular Benefits

Cremini mushrooms have shown to provide remarkable cardiovascular benefits that can help prevent cardiovascular disease and are particularly proven to protect the aorta.

Daily consumption for several months has also indicated the cremini can help lower cholesterol, LDL cholesterol, and triglycerides.

The cremini mushrooms are also excellent sources of vitamins B2, B3, and B5 (pantothenic acid) B6, and folate.

Anti-Cancer Benefits

The benefits of cremini mushrooms for immune support, and inflammation support. They also aid in preventing and fighting cancer.

Preparation and Cooking

Raw Agaricus bisporus do contain small amounts of toxins that are reduced by heat so cooking mushrooms before eating is recommended.

White Button

White Button: Agaricus bisporus

The white button mushroom, is a common grocery store item in the produce department and relatively inexpensive. This "table mushroom" is so common that is the U.S., the typical consumption per person is about two pounds annually. They also grow wild in grasslands all over the world. The button mushroom is white though turn brown when bruised.

Health and Medicinal Benefits

There is verification that white button mushrooms can enhance the immune system and battle cancer. They have B vitamins, selenium, potassium, and protein as well as other essential vitamins and minerals.

Note: In nature, confusing the Agaricus bisporus with poisonous mushrooms such as the fatal death cap mushroom is easy. Make sure you have an experienced person along who can identify good from poisonous mushrooms if you go mushroom hunting.

Preparation and Cooking

White button mushrooms are flavorful and easy to cook. The Agaricus bisporus should be washed thoroughly and wrapped in paper for storage. They will last about a week in refrigeration which is longer than most mushrooms.

These mushrooms are cooked with meat, fish, poultry, or as a pizza topping. They are marinated, skewered, grilled and sautéed.

Growing White Buttons

White button mushrooms grow best on compost and kits are highly successful. These will begin fruiting within a week or so. Button mushrooms are grown on a compost substrate.

Portobellos

Portobello: Agaricus bisporus

The Portobello is the mature version of the cremini or white button. Growing button mushrooms indoors is fairly easy as the common white buttons and portobello or cremini (baby portobellos).

They are tasty and a good kit will yield your crop within three weeks and fruit for as much as eight more weeks.

Enoki

Enoki: Flammulina velutipes

The Enoki mushroom is also called the enokitake, enokidake, winter mushroom, furry foot, nametake, yuki-motase, golden needle, winter mushroom, snow puff and velvet stem mushroom.

Enokis are commercially grown and found in the wild in clusters growing on aspen, elm and willow trees. The cultivated Enoki mushroom looks different than the wild grown form as they are much larger and have a burnt orange color. This is due to the fact that this mushroom has morphologically sensitivity light and carbon dioxide. On the other hand when cultivated the Enoki are almost pure white with long stems and small caps.

Health and Medicinal Benefits

Enoki mushrooms are low-fat and have protein, carbohydrates, dietary fiber, and an excellent source of niacin, iron and potassium. The Chinese and Japanese claim the Enoki mushroom prevents and cures liver diseases and stomach ulcers.

Preparation and Cooking

Enoki mushrooms have a mild flavor and are small and white with tall stalks and are commonly sold in a bunch. They are popular for use in salads; noodle and stir fry dishes and go well with soba noodles, lemongrass, herbs, soy, and seafood or poultry.

Growing Enoki Mushrooms

Enoki mushrooms caps are between one to two inches diameter and can be five inches tall with a white, light cream color, or reddish brown. Enoki is fairly easy to grow, needing a humid environment and warm temperatures on hardwood sawdust medium.

How to Grow Mushrooms at Home

Step One

Hardwood sawdust medium must be inoculated with Enoki mushroom sterilized spawn usually in a syringe.

Step Two

Enoki mushrooms must be kept in a warm environment to spawn. The humidity needs to be close to 100 per cent and the temperature should be 72 to 78 degrees Fahrenheit (22-25 degrees Celsius). preferably with increased exposure to CO_2. Spawning should occur in about two to four weeks.

Step Three

After spawning the temperature is lowered to 50 to 55 degrees Fahrenheit (10-12 degrees Celsius) to encourage growth. Reduce the amount of CO_2 exposure to 80 to 90 percent.

Step Four

Harvest your Enoki mushrooms in bunches or bouquets to guard their delicate structure. The substrate might be able to produce one more crop.

Maitake Mushroom

Maitake: Grifola frondosa

This mushroom, also known as the "hen of the woods", "sheep's head", "king of mushrooms" and "cloud mushroom," is edible and flavorful. Maitake means "dancing mushroom" in Japanese and is a polypore so it has no gills and releases spores from small pores. Grifola frondosa grow in the wild appearing at the base of oak trees and some others in the United States and Canada and in Japan, China, and Europe.

The caps are in curvy layers that sprout from a large tubular structure underground. The mushroom can measure several few feet across and weigh as much as 40 to 50 pounds (18-22 Kilograms).

Health Benefits and Medicinal Effects

In Japan, the maitake mushroom has been used for years as a powerful medicinal mushroom. Similar to other polypore has polysaccharides that motivate the immune system.

A polysaccharide is a complex carbohydrate consisting of tinier sugar molecules that stabilize blood pressure. Specific polysaccharides, such as beta-D-glucans, are believed to arouse the immune system against cancer. A glucan extract is the maitake D-fraction or MD-fraction.

In addition to helping fight cancer, research for the benefits of other conditions include:

- diabetes
- HIV/AIDS
- high cholesterol
- high blood pressure

Maitake supplements are available as an extract of the D or MD fraction, or powdered capsules.

Preparation and Cooking

Maitake mushroom caps can be stir fried, baked, sauteed, stuffed, or used in tea.

Growing Maitake Mushrooms

Maitake mushrooms are luscious and, although they are desirable for culinary and medicinal purposes, they are not common in grocery stores. You can grow maitake mushrooms indoors, but keep in mind they are finicky and need accurate light levels, temperature, and humidity.

Step One

Buy maitake spawn as a liquid, grain, sawdust or wooden plugs. If you are fabricating your own substrate from scratch or for commercial operations, you will want the liquid spawn.

Step Two

Create a substrate with a blend of about half to three fourths sawdust and hardwood chips. The remainder should be a grain such as wheat bran and a small amount (approximately 1 per cent) of sugar. You can also add about ten per cent top soil from a place where hardwoods grow. This is blended in burlap or plastic bags with vent holes. Slowly put in small amounts of calcium, lime or gypsum until the substrate reaches a pH level of five and a half to six and a half percent.

Step Three

Inoculate the substrate with the spawn liquid, sawdust, or grain. You can drill small holes in a log and insert the plugs.

Step Four

Your project should be in a room without any direct sunlight and with some air flow and venting with a temperature of 60 to 70 degrees Fahrenheit (15-21 degrees Celsius) and about 60 to 75 per cent humidity can be maintained.

Step Five

Your maitake mushrooms should fruit and unfurled like a flower within three to four months for harvesting. Mushroom caps ought to be upright and should have a fresh earthy aroma. When mushrooms have a fishy odor or have released spores, they are not suitable for eating.

Lion's Mane

Lion's Mane: Hericium erinaceus

Lion's mane is pure white and grows in several strands clustered in a round shape with a rigid texture. They can be 6 inches or larger in diameter. They grow wild in the southern area of the United States usually on dead oak, walnut, beech, sycamore, and maple trees.

Health Benefits and Medicinal Effects

Lion's Mane mushroom has been highly prized in China and used to treat digestion issues as well as esophagus and stomach cancer. Research results show that the mushroom contains polysaccharides that stimulate the immune system and increase white blood cell count to facilitate healing. Lion's Mane has also demonstrated abilities to assist in controlling blood sugar and cholesterol levels. There is no evidence of any side effects from this mushroom or risk of toxicity.

Another area of current research is in the mushroom's potential to help battle dementia and Alzheimer's disease.

[4]Hirokazu Kawagishi of Shizoka University Japan, a documented authority on Lion's Mane has confirmed the extraordinary ability of this mushroom to stimulate the synthesis of Nerve Growth Factor (NGF). A deficiency of NGF is thought to be a chief cause of Alzheimer's disease.

Preparation and Cooking

Lion's mane is a delicacy in the East. This mushroom has a taste that resembles seafood. Lion's mane must be cooked slowly to retain the flavor and any spices should be added when almost done cooking.

---

[4] http://www.ultimateimmune.com/articles/lions-mane.php

Growing Lion's Mane Mushrooms

You can purchase Lion's mane mushroom kits in plastic bags for indoor growing. Normal room temperature is recommended and mist twice a day.

Harvest when the spines are elongated but prior to softening of the fruiting mass and any development of a yellow color.

Paddy Straw

Image Source: bestspores.com

Paddy Straw: (Volvariella violaceae)

Paddy straw mushroom or Chinese Mushroom is commercially grown in Asia on rice straw. This is a dark colored mushroom used in numerous Asian dishes.

They have a markedly appealing taste. Their unique shape is easy to recognize and is sold at grocery stores canned, fresh, or dried. The mushrooms grow surrounded by a sack and can be left on or removed at harvest or at time of cooking.

Health Benefits and Medicinal Effects

Paddy Straw mushrooms are thought to help mend damage caused by auto-immune disease. They also offer many of the nutritional benefits associated with other mushrooms.

Preparation and Cooking

These small bite size mushrooms have a meaty texture and are a great addition to vegetable dishes, stir fry, chop suey, chow mein, soups, and sauces.

Growing Paddy Straw Mushrooms

The Paddy Straw mushroom's natural habitat is tropical so growing the mushroom in warm indoor environments is suitable. This mushroom is typically grown in paddy straw that is dried and tied in bundles and then soaked in water for 12 to 16 hours. The Paddy Straw spawn is also created on grains or millets.

Mushrooms usually appear within two weeks after beds are spawned and will fruit for a week or so. Due to their delicate make up, they only last a few days after harvest - even when refrigerated.

Shiitake Mushrooms

Shiitake: (Lentinula edodes)

Shiitakes (she-ta-keys) have been called the "king of mushrooms" and they can grow to three or four-inches in diameter. They have an umbrella-shape dark brown color. These brown mushrooms have meaty consistency and small white spots or flecks. They have a rich full and even smoky flavor and are popular for cooking flavorful dishes. These mushrooms are also popular dried to use in cooking as well as for health and medicinal reasons. Shiitakes have a long history of culinary and medicinal uses by Native Americans and Asian societies.

This mushroom gets to claim the third spot for most widely produced mushroom in the world. Production of Shiitake in the U.S. has been occurring for over twenty years and is growing faster than any of the other specialty mushrooms.

Health and Medicinal Benefits

Shiitake are often called medicinal mushrooms because of their medical use in oriental medicine. The results of extensive studies show these mushrooms decrease blood pressure, lower cholesterol levels, protect the immune system, and possess anti-tumor properties. Shiitake mushrooms contain lentinan, a natural anti-tumor compound and are a great source of vitamin D. Shiitake mushrooms also exhibit antiviral that work against HIV, hepatitis, and the common cold. In addition to vitamin D and minerals, Shiitake also have A, B, B12, and C. Shiitake contains every one of the eight essential amino acids. The amino acids in this mushroom are in better scope than milk, meat, eggs or even soy beans.

The medicinal benefits of the Shiitake are confirmed and consist of antiviral and antifungal effects with the ability to lower cholesterol and high blood pressure.

Most medicinal research studies on Shiitake mushrooms have been conducted with extracts in laboratories which are not the same as the Shiitake mushroom consumed as a food. There is subsequently an abundance of medicinal information on shiitake mushrooms extract and less about the benefits in human consumption as a food. Yet the information that is available is apparent and shows the Shiitake mushrooms have distinct and extraordinary health benefits.

Immune Support

The immune support evidence for Shittake mushrooms is impressive. The extracts have proven to have most of the medicinal benefits.

The extraordinary mixture of antioxidants in shiitake mushrooms along with a support for the immune systems, open up possibilities for the potential of protection from a number of issues such as rheumatoid arthritis (RA).

Cardiovascular Benefits

The cardiovascular benefits of Shiitake mushrooms have been recognized in three fundamental areas including cholesterol reduction, the interaction between our cardiovascular system and our immune system, and cardiovascular benefits that involve antioxidant support.

Shiitake mushrooms are rich in three key antioxidant minerals: manganese, selenium, and zinc and some uncommon phytonutrient antioxidants.

Anti-Cancer Benefits

As mentioned, research has been performed on medicinal extracts from shiitake mushrooms than the whole food. There is evidence that certain elements of the shiitake mushroom help block tumor growth.

Growing Shiitake Mushrooms

You can grow Shiitake mushrooms at home on blocks of sterilized sawdust. The blocks can be enhanced with cottonseed meal. You can inoculate logs and grow Shiitake mushrooms in a humid warm area such as a basement. Growing shiitake on logs might produce the best mushroom though sawdust creates more surface areas from the particles for more potential colonization.

Shiitake mushroom kits are easy to grow indoors between 55ºF to 75ºF. A kit will commonly yield two to three pounds in just a few months, fruiting every few weeks.

Oyster Mushrooms

Oyster: (Pleurotus)

Oyster mushrooms come in a variety of species and forms, but the Pleurotus ostreatus and Pleurotus pulmonarius are popular for growing. A member of the Pleurotaceae family, oyster mushrooms can grow in the wild in clusters on logs, tree stumps, and deciduous tree trunks with a cap width of one to six inches and a stalk length up to 1¼ inches (2-15 cm) and about ¾ inch round (2-3 cm wide).

The oyster mushroom's native habitat includes deciduous hardwood and conifer trees as a decomposer. They can be found in forests the world over.

The popular oyster mushroom gets the name from having a taste and texture similar to oysters. Considered a delicacy, the wild oyster mushrooms have better flavor than the commercially cultivated ones often found in the grocery stores. However, the popularity of this fungus has caused production to increase at a rate of more than ten per cent annually. However this desired culinary mushroom is not only found on dinner plates around the world, it serves to dispose of waste plastics and petroleum spills through digestion. Oyster mushrooms can degrade environmental toxins and help clean polluted areas.

Health and Medicinal Benefits

Oyster mushrooms are currently being researched for being a potential defense against HIV because of the high anti-oxidant compounds this species contains.

Oyster mushrooms are rich in protein, B vitamins, are cholesterol free, and contain substantial amounts of the cholesterol-lowering molecule lovastatin.

Oyster mushrooms have a reputation for being the easiest to grow, abundantly nutritious and medicinally valuable.

Preparation and Cooking

Oyster caps are scrumptious when sautéed.

Oysters fluctuate in flavor although are generally milder than the shiitake mushroom.

Oyster mushrooms are a highly desirable culinary item, although they are not common in grocery stores because of their fragile texture makes them a challenge to ship.

Oyster mushrooms must be cooked before eating as they contain a protein known as "ostreolysin," which can be toxic.

Growing Oyster Mushrooms

Oyster kits are typically a collection of sticky white mycelium wholly colonized, as well as a small wheat or oat straw column. This is packaged in a plastic bag with holes.

Oyster mushrooms thrive in high humidity and need misting several times a day. The "blue dolphin" is best kept below 65°F (18 degrees Celsius). The "golden oyster" has yellow fruits and the "white oyster" is considered the easiest to cultivate.

When they receive the right care, temperature and humidity, a tower kit will explode with these mushrooms.

Kits will frequently fruit two times. Then you can put the mycelium in a compost heap to grow more.

Blending the mycelium with damp sawdust, coffee grounds and some straw, and placing this in paper board milk cartons with a few holes the sides, and then putting these in plastic bags to remain in the dark for a month or two, can produce more oysters. Oyster mushrooms on commercial farms are grown on columns of sterilized straw hung from ceilings.

Wine caps

Images Source: urbpan.livejournal.com

Also known as King Stropharia, Godzilla, and the Garden Giant, these mushrooms have a large cap that grows to be as large as five inches (12 cm) across with a reddish-brown tone or wine color it ages. Popular in Europe this mushroom grows naturally in forests in the United States, Europe, New Zealand and Japan.

Health and Medicinal Benefits

Wine caps contain many of the common nutrients found in mushrooms and it is believed to promote healthy skin, as well as prevent hangnails and blisters.

Preparation and Cooking

This mushroom can be baked, fried, stuffed, added to sauce, and is good when stir fried in butter and some lemon juice, wine, nutmeg, or fennel. Cooking with onion or garlic is not recommended.

Growing Wine caps

While most people grow wine caps in outdoor gardens they can also be cultivated indoors. A substrate of sawdust and pasteurized straw with a covering of rich soil and Douglas fir and alder woodchips inoculated with spawn will work best. Kits can fruit repeatedly after three to four weeks of dormancy between fruiting.

Reishi Mushrooms

Reishi: Ganoderma lucidum

Reishi mushrooms are polypores (no gills) and there is a flat area underneath the cap where the spores are released. The Ganoderma lucidum come in red, purple, green, white, yellow, and black. The Reishi looks similar to a flower with the texture of wood.

69

Reishi is known as the mushroom of immortality in China and is also called the herb of spiritual potency. They have a long history of medicinal use in China dating back over 2,000 years. While their original habitat was in China, Japan, and Korea, this mushroom is grown on hardwoods such as maple, oaks, and elms around the world. The reishi is in the saprotroph category with some people also classifying this one as a parasite.

Health and Medicinal Benefits

The red reishi mushroom is said to have the most healing properties. The supplements are sake with no known harmful side effects. Reishi mushrooms have numerous health benefits such as:

- regulating blood pressure
- stimulating liver actions
- fighting the effects of stress

And treating:

- insomnia
- gastric ulcers
- neurasthenia
- arthritis
- nephritis
- asthma
- bronchitis

- hypertension
- neuromuscular disorders
- myasthenia gravis
- muscular dystrophy

Anti-inflammatory, useful for reducing symptoms of rheumatoid arthritis

- Immune system up-regulation
- Normalization of blood cholesterol levels and blood pressure
- Reduction of prostate-related urinary symptoms in men

Reishi mushrooms supplements are taken for:

- Allergies
- Anxiety
- Asthma
- Bronchitis
- Cancer, particularly leukemia
- Chronic fatigue syndrome
- Flu prevention
- HIV/AIDS
- High blood pressure
- High cholesterol
- Inflammatory conditions
- Insomnia

- Diabetes
- Hepatitis
- Radiation poisoning

The effects of this mushroom are cumulative and can take several weeks or more to see.

Preparation and Cooking

Reishi mushrooms are eaten and drank in a variety of ways:

- In soup: sautéed in olive oil, salt, and seasonings.
- Grilled: as side dish.
- Dried reishi mushrooms can be found whole ground into a powder.
- Reishi tea is made from ground mushrooms.
- The dried powder is also used to create "reishi spirits".

Growing Reishi Mushrooms

Growing Reishi mushrooms takes meticulousness. It is not too complicated, as long as attention is given to temperature and humidity. Grow kits are available and recommended for beginners.

Growing reishi mushrooms indoors can be done anytime of the year with humidity maintained and a temperature usually less than 70 degrees F (21 degrees Celsius). Most reishi mushrooms will have a red or brown cap unless carbon dioxide levels are too high. Then instead of a cap small fingers will form.

Turkey Tail

Turkey tail: (Stereum ostrea)

Turkey tail mushrooms grow in bunches of leathery, thin layers, often in many colors, hence their name. They can be found in the wild on stumps and logs of deciduous trees.

The cap is usually one to four inches in diameter and no stalk is present. While the colors on the cap make the turkey tail easy to spot, there is also the false turkey tail (Stereum ostrea) that has a smooth underside.

Image Source: http://www.etsy.com/listing/88164672/turkey-tail-mushroom-growing-kit-for

Health and Medicinal Benefits

Turkey tail mushrooms have been treating a variety of woes for centuries in Asia, Europe, and North America. Turkey tail is used to boost the immune system and for liver cancer and jaundice.

Studies show turkey tail mushrooms could be an effective addition to chemotherapeutic and radiation treatments.

Preparation and Cooking

Turkey tail is typically ground for use as a tea or in soup.

Growing Turkey Tail

While you can grow turkey tail mushrooms at home in a terrarium, they are difficult to grow and not recommended for beginners. Mushrooms can vary considerably, dependent on the culture, the growing methods and production system. The mycellium can be grown in a tightly controlled environment.

4. Indoor Mushroom Farming

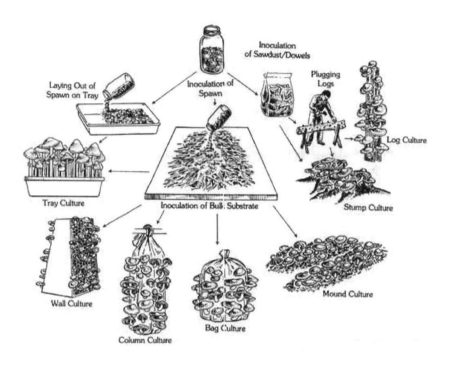

Image Source: fungi.com

Choose Your Fungus

While the most popular mushrooms grown indoors are included in this book, there are hundreds of edible mushrooms you can grow indoors. The oyster mushroom is great for beginning growers. Oyster mushrooms are easy exotic mushrooms to grow and you can use an assortment of products for a substrate such as straw and wood chips, cardboard, and coffee grounds. These common substrates will help you succeed in getting the best crop yields.

If you are considering growing mushrooms to make money, oyster mushrooms can bring top dollar and are in high demand in many areas. You can grow an oyster mushroom in about six weeks. As with most mushrooms, oysters are best when freshly picked. As previously mentioned, if you cannot sell them immediately, you can dry them and they will last several months.

Here are some questions to help you choose:

1. Which of the mushrooms do you want to grow? Check the market and the temperature ranges for fruiting.
2. Will you be growing for your own consumption or potential profit?
3. Do you have a space with the appropriate environment for growing the mushroom you would like?
4. Can you obtain mushroom spawn or a kit of the species you want to grow?
5. If not using a kit, what kind of substrate would you need to be able to grow the desired mushrooms?

When you choose the type of mushroom you want to grow, review all the specific growing requirements of that species.

You can then purchase your spawn from a garden center or online. You can find numerous websites selling spawn and these kits will produce a load of mushrooms.

Kits

Mushroom kits are available for getting started growing indoors. The kits have all you need to grow mushrooms counting the spores, or spawns, substrate and so on.

They are easy to use and usually include a cardboard box or perforated bag that has been inoculated for cultivating the specific mushroom. These kits usually contain the ingredients to produce multiple crops for two to four months. The cost at this time is typically less than $35. And the kits are in gardening stores, some organic grocery stores, and available online.

You can also grow mushrooms in sterile jars. Fill the jars with your substrate or medium and then spread the spores. Regulating the humidity and temperature can be easy in a jar.

Environment

Each species of mushroom has different growing and environmental requirements. Oysters or button mushrooms are great for beginning growers.

Cleanliness

All mushrooms need a clean environment to avoid contamination. If you are not using a kit and creating your own substrate, pasteurize the straw to remove any possible contamination. Submerge the straw in hot water at least 140 degrees F for one hour. Drain the substrate and let cool. Place the straw into the plastic bag and then spread the spawn on top until the bag is full.

Temperature and Humidity

Set up your kit where the temperature is stable. Depending on the climate where you live and your accommodations, you might need to experiment with different locations.

Most mushrooms thrive in cool and damp conditions. The humidity should be 70 to 80 percent and the temperature between 55 and 70 degrees Fahrenheit (12-21 degrees Celsius). These conditions can be found in many bathroom, kitchens, and basements.

Moisture is critical for crops. Constant humidity is essential for the mushrooms to develop and grow. Mushrooms will not grow in air that is too dry. In most climates, the mist from a spray bottle with water two or three times a day is sufficient. In a dry climate, you will need to spray the mushrooms more often. Do not overspray by making the cardboard soggy or wet.

Light

Keep them out of direct light by growing in a cabinet, closet or other dark area. Some indirect light is needed for some mushrooms such as oysters while others such as the white buttons and cremini must have total darkness. (Exposure to light can result in brown caps.)

Air

Mushrooms need air. Even a closet or cabinet will need some ventilation to prevent an accumulation of carbon dioxide (CO_2). Too much CO_2 can slow mushroom production to a crawl or stop growth altogether. A fan can be enough for air circulation.

Equipment

Even if you purchase a growing kit you will need:

- electric fan
- spray mist bottle
- cooking oil spray
- bleach

Growing in a Plastic Bag

Submerge the straw for substrate in hot water at least 140 degrees F (60 degrees Celsius) for one hour. Drain the substrate and let cool. Place the straw into the plastic bag and then spread the spawn on top until the bag is full.

Tie the top of the bag with a tie made of metal. Perforate the bag all over to allow air circulation. Place the bag in a warm room for about 2 weeks. The bag will become white as it colonizes with mycelium growth.

When the bag is fully colonized fruiting should start in a few days. You can move the bag to a cooler with area high humidity during this period to encourage fruiting.

You can tell when to harvest by seeing the veil that attaches the cap to the stem start tearing. Oyster mushrooms must be harvested before the caps unfurl and release spores. Rotate the bag each day to spot mushrooms ready for harvest. Lightly turn and pull mushrooms to remove leaving any broken stems behind.

Substrates

Images Source: http://www.smithbrosmulch.com

While spawn can grow mushrooms, you will produce more and better mushrooms when growing in a substrate such as straw, cardboard, logs, orwood chips. Compost that is made up of a combination of straw, corncobs, gypsum, cotton and cocoa seed hulls and nitrogen supplements is better and more commonly used by commercial growers. Nitrogen supplements and gypsum are added.

Mushrooms need nitrogen and carbohydrates to grow. Mushrooms metabolize carbohydrates from the substrate into glucose. This moves through the mycelium and provides nourishment. Concentration in the substrate should be about 1 percent and never over 2 percent.

Bulk substrates include:

- Wood chips or sawdust
- Mulched straw (wheat, rice or other)
- Straw bedded horse or poultry manure
- Corncobs
- Waste or recycled paper
- Coffee grounds
- Nut and seed hulls
- Cottonseed hulls
- Cocoa bean hulls
- Cottonseed meal
- Soybean meal
- Brewer's grain
- Ammonium nitrate
- Urea

When spreading out the straw substrate to cool, always make sure all surfaces have been cleaned with a 10% bleach solution. Again, wash your hands thoroughly *before and after* working with substrate and spawn.

Pests

You can spray the box top flaps with cooking oil spray to stop insects from getting to your mushrooms. There are also nematodes which are tiny worms that eat plants and fungi. Oyster mushrooms are not affected as the mycelium is carnivorous and eats bugs.

Why People Fail

Growing mushrooms is not difficult when you follow the proper procedures and have the correct knowledge. Meeting the needs of mushrooms require attention to environment and conditions.

Environment

One common reason people fail to grow mushrooms indoors is they do not keep humidity levels adequate for growth. Unless you have a humidifier (and do not over saturate) you must remember to spray your mushrooms with water every day.

Cleanliness

Another fail point for growing mushrooms is sterilization and cleanliness. Maintaining a high level of cleanliness to avoid contaminants is critical. All surfaces and items that might come in contact with spawn substrates or containers should be cleaned with a 10% bleach solution. Hands should be washed *before and after* working with your mushroom production.

Cautions

Pets

99% of mushrooms pose no issues and have little or no toxicity. There are mushrooms that are toxic to animals. Just to be safe, take extra precaution to keep your mushrooms where pets cannot access them.

If you suspect that your pet has eaten a toxic mushroom, contact your veterinarian, pet emergency hospital, or the animal poison control center. Let them know what type of mushroom your pet has consumed. If in the wild and you cannot identify the fungus bring a sample or picture along to the emergency center.

Pests and Diseases

Mushroom production can be harmed by parasitic insects, bacteria and other fungi. The sciarid fly or phorid fly can lay their eggs in the substrate. These hatch into worms and spoil mushrooms at any phase of growth. There are pesticides and sanitizing agents available to fight pests.

Mold

Trichoderma green mold, as well as others, can significantly affect your mushroom growing. If mold appears in or on your kit or substrate, you will need to halt production and throw out all affected material, and clean the area thoroughly before starting over.

Preserving Mushrooms

Mushrooms are at their peak when harvested and that is when you should eat or sell them. Mushrooms harvested at the right time can be preserved for later.

If you cannot sell your mushrooms or you want to save them, as stated earlier, you can freeze or dry them. These methods will preserve your mushrooms for months.

5. Basics of Larger Scale Mushroom Farming

Image Source: http://infranetlab.org

The following six steps are relevant for larger scale mushroom farming and the principles and much of the information is relevant to small scale indoor growing. The more you know about mushroom growing the better your chances of success and of producing better mushrooms and crop yields.

Materials used for mushroom compost include wheat straw or synthetics. In this case the synthetics can still be natural ingredients, as this label refers to any compost that does not contain horse manure. Synthetic compost is typically made from hay and crushed corncobs. You need to add nitrogen supplements and a conditioning agent called gypsum to either compost.

You might not be able to obtain corn cobs at a reasonable price. There are substitutes for corn cobs you can use such as cocoa bean hulls, shredded hardwood bark, cottonseed hulls, and neutralized grape pumice.

Straw and hay degrade and hold moisture during composting. When this happens clumping can occur that prevent air circulation, causing an anaerobic situation.

The preparation of compost is done in two steps and often called Phase I and Phase II composting.

- Step 1: Composting Phase 1
- Step 2: Composting Phase 2
- Step 3: Spawning
- Step 4: Casing
- Step 5: Pinning
- Step 6: Cropping

Step I: Making Mushroom Compost

Compost preparation is frequently accomplished outdoors however can be done inside. For larger scale growing a wharf or concrete slab is what you need to build the compost pile. This compost pile ought to measure five to six feet across by as long as you need. The sides need to be rigid and dense, thought the middle needs to be loose during this step.

A compost turner will help aerate and water your elements. Blend and wet your ingredients while you pile them in a rectangular stack. Again, it is important to stress that the sides should be tight and the middle loose.

Spread nitrogen supplements and gypsum over the top. Add gypsum at the start at a rate of 40 pounds per one ton of dry ingredients in order to reduce the greasiness that naturally occurs. Gypsum also increases the clumping of some chemicals in the compost as they stick to the straw or hay. An advantage of this event is that air can permeate the pile more easily. Without enough air, harmful chemical compounds formed, which degrade the compost for growing mushrooms.

Six Steps of Mushroom Cultivation

Step	Time Period	Temperature	Information
1. Phase I composting	1 to 2 weeks		Regulate water and NH_3 content. Add fertilizer / supplements
2. Phase II composting or pasteurization	1 to 3 weeks depending on method		Reduce potentially harmful bacteria through composting, or heat sterilization. Remove unwanted NH_3.
3. Spawning and growth	2 to 3 weeks	75°F; to 80°F; Keep below 80°F to prevent damage to mycelia	Add starter culture. Allow mycelium to grow through substrate and form a colony.
4. Casing	2-3 weeks		Add top covering to the substrate. Fertilize with nitrogen to increase crop yields.
5. Pinning	About 3 weeks		Mushrooms can now be seen growing. Temperature, humidity and CO_2 will determine number of pins, and mushroom size
6. Cropping	Repeated over 7-10 day cycles		Harvest

There are several nitrogen supplements including brewer's grain, peanuts, soybean seed meal, cotton, and chicken manure. Nitrogen supplements increase the nitrogen content to one and a half per cent with horse manure or a bit more, one and seven tenths per cent for synthetic, calculated on a dry weight basis.

When the compost is wet the aerobic fermentation begins as microorganisms grow and reproduce naturally. During this process heat, ammonia, and carbon dioxide are released. The activity of microorganisms, heat, and heat releasing chemical reactions in the compost best convert the materials into a food source for mushrooms while preventing the growth of other fungi and bacteria. This process needs moisture, oxygen, nitrogen, and carbohydrates to happen so water and supplements are added every so often. Oxygen is supplied during aeration when the compost is turned. Ammonium nitrate or urea is needed to start synthetic compost to nitrogen.

Turn and water the pile every two days when the pile is hot (between about 145° to 170°F (62 -76°C). This will water, aerate, and mix the components. How often you need to turn the pile will depend on the condition of the material in the beginning and how long you need to reach temperatures above 145°F (62°C).

Adding water in the right amounts is a must as over watering prevents oxygen from occupying the pore space, and not enough water can prohibit the development of bacteria and fungi.

Watering is usually done until leaching at the initial turning. At this point, add only a bit of water periodically during composting. Before Phase II, composting at final turning water can be added liberally. The amounts and elements of water, nutrition, microbial activity, and temperature, are directly related to the total process and referred to as the Law of Limiting Factors.

This step lasts from 1 to 2 weeks and you might smell an ammonia odor and moldy smell during composting. Ammonia is present at higher temperatures over 155 degrees F.

Compost pile temperatures can climb to 170 to 180 degrees F at the time of the second and third turnings.

Signs that this Phase is complete:

- Compost color: dark brown
- Texture: soft, bendable straws
- Moisture content: 68 to 74 percent
- Smell: strong ammonia odor

Step II: Completing the Compost

Step II involves pasteurization and eradicating ammonia. P Pasteurization will get rid of insects, pest fungi, or other pests. The ammonia created during step I with a level higher than 0.07 percent is frequently lethal to mushroom spawn. Phase II composting is about removing ammonia and maintaining the optimum temperature for the organisms to grow and reproduce as they use carbohydrates and nitrogen. This Step is also for eradicating any pests through a pasteurization cycle.

There are several production systems for mushroom farming.

Zone Production System

In this system, wood trays are filled with compost. These trays are kept in stacks in an environmentally controlled room. The trays are moved as needed during the growing

Shelf or Bed Production System

In this system, the compost is placed in beds that remain where they are.

Bulk Production System

In the bulk mushroom production system compost is put in a cinder block container with floor drains designed for growing mushrooms.

The compost needs to be uniform in depth.

A high temperature for pasteurization of 145°F for 6 hours is reached by the heat generated naturally or by introducing steam into the room. Then the compost cools over a week or two at about 2° to 3°F (about 1-2 °C)each day until all ammonia is gone.

Step III: Spawning

The compost now needs to be inoculated with mushroom spawn. Mushrooms are grown from mycelium. In this step spawn is spread and then methodically mixed into the compost. The rate of spawning is in term of a quart per so many square feet of surface. A quart (4 cups) per 10 square feet is sought-after. The rate is also now and then articulated as spawn weight versus compost weight. In this case you would want a two percent spawning rate.

This step typically takes three to four weeks depending on several factors including the spawning rate, moisture content and temperature, and the compost type and quality.

Step IV: Casing

Casing is a topping of clay-loam soil, a mixture of peat moss with limestone powder, or reclaimed compost. Casing serves as a water reservoir and for rhizomorphs to form. Rhizomorphs are like strings and appear as the mycelium grows together. Casing is pasteurized to prevent introducing any insects or contaminates to the compost. Then the casing is spread evenly over the compost.

Humidity is kept high and compost temperature is usually maintained at 75°F (23°C) for four or five 5 days after casing. The compost will soon show small mushroom pins.

Step V: Pinning

Pinning is the most complex step for mushroom farmers. They must get the right combination of carbon dioxide (CO_2), temperature, and humidity to get mushrooms to fruit.

Image Source: gardendrum.com

When carbon dioxide levels are lowered to 0.08 percent or lower pins will develop. Pins will grow in the button stage and eventually become mushrooms. Mushrooms will be ready to harvest about three weeks after casing. Air and water amounts in this period are directly related to the mushroom quality and crop yield.

Step VI: Cropping

Mushrooms are harvested in cycles usually in five to ten day periods in a rhythmic fashion. Cropping or harvesting is usually a six to seven week period though some can last much longer. These periods are also known as flush, break, or bloom.

Air temperature in the cropping period is usually set at 57° to 62°F (13-16 °C). Outside air is introduced for temperature control and carbon dioxide removal. The amount of fresh air needed depends on the amount of mushrooms, the area of surface, the amount of compost and the condition.

Mushrooms are watered two or three times a week during cropping.

Harvested mushrooms have to be refrigerated at 35° to 45°F (1-7°C). Mushrooms are packaged in perforated material or a paper bag to prolong shelf life.

Conclusion
A production cycle will take about fifteen 15 weeks from composting to harvesting. Basically, yield should be from 0 to 4 pounds (around 1kg) per square foot. The factors that

affect yield include how the humidity and temperature were controlled, outside influences such as pests and so on.

Learning mushroom growing basics and understanding the natural biological rhythms of growing mushrooms is a great advantage for achieving consistent success.

Certified Organic

Health gurus advocate consuming organically grown mushrooms due to the fact that mushrooms can soak up contaminants from the air and soil.

[5]At this time no organic certification standards are in place exclusively for mushroom production. There are organic standards for general food production that apply to growing organic mushrooms.

---

[5] http://www.whfoods.com/genpage.php?tname=foodspice&dbid=97

Appendix

Small Scale Mushroom Cultivation, <FAO.org>

Shiitake Log Production, <https://store.aces.edu>

The Mushroom Council offers excellent research and production information for mushroom growers. <http://mushroomcouncil.org/>

The University of California Small Farm Program
The potential for mushroom production on small farms and online publication: Mushrooms: A Small Scale Agriculture alternative.
<http://www.sfc.ucdavis.edu/>

The National Sustainable Agriculture Information Service (ATTRA) offers comprehensive information on mushroom production and sales on their Mushroom Cultivation and Marketing page. <https://attra.ncat.org/>

Reference for Mushroom Growers from Penn State University <http://extension.psu.edu/plants/vegetable-fruit/mushrooms>

GardenGuides.com: Low Cost Mushroom Production at Home. <http://www.gardenguides.com >

How to Grow Mushrooms at Home

The Mushroom Growers Newsletter
<http://www.mushroomcompany.com>

University of Maryland Extension: Shiitake.
<http://www.naturalresources.umd.edu/Publications/html/shiitake.html>

Mushroom Production Directory lists companies who sell supplies, and farms that produce edible mushrooms.
<http://www.hotfrog.com/Products/Mushroom-Production>

Gourmet Mushrooms and Mushroom Products: mushroom growing kits, spawn, books, and other supplies.
<http://www.gmushrooms.com >

Gourmet Mushrooms Inc. : equipment and information about mushroom production.
<http://www.gourmetmushroomsinc.com>

Shroomery: Mushroom production.
<http://www.shroomery.org >

MycoWeb: Lots of great scientific information, pictures, recipes, articles, links, and much more and much more…
<http://www.mykoweb.com/>

Tom Volk's Fungi Page:< http://www.tomvolkfungi.net/>

FungiPhoto.com: <http://www.fungiphoto.com/>

How to Grow Mushrooms at Home

<http://www.rogersmushrooms.com/>

Best Practices for Mushroom Production and Marketing
<http://americanmushroom.org/>

Community Awareness Committee (CAC)
<http://www.mushroomfarmcommunity.org/>

Mushroom Compost Website
<http://www.mushroomcompost.org/>

The Mushroom Information Center
<http://www.mushroominfo.com/>

The Mushroom Council
<http://mushroomcouncil.org/>

The Penn State Mushroom Spawn Laboratory
   This site has been developed to serve as a reference for Mushroom Growers by Penn State University. It contains the Mushroom Facts Sheet as well as many useful links.
<http://plantpath.psu.edu/facilities/mushroom/cultures-spawn>

International Society for Mushroom Science
   ISMS serves to disseminate information on new

developments and science of mushrooms and to stimulate the exchange of ideas among growers and scientists around the world. <http://www.isms.biz/>

USDA's Economic Research Service - Mushroom Statistics Statistical information on this site provides almost every statistic ever compiled about the mushroom industry from 1966-2009. The information is presented in tables gathered from the USDA, the Census Bureau, Statistics Canada and the Food and Agriculture Organization of the United States. <http://usda.mannlib.cornell.edu>

Mushroom Education Packet
Workbook for instructing school age children all about mushrooms.
<http://www.americanmushroom.org/workbook.pdf>

The Mushroom Growers' Newsletter
Contains information of interest to commercial mushroom growers, as well as links to other sites.
< http://www.mushroomcompany.com>

Fungus of the Month
<http://botit.botany.wisc.edu/toms_fungi/fotm.html>

Home Cultivation
Paul Stamets, leader in the home cultivation field —
supplies, books, kits, everything a mushroom cultivator
needs.

Paul Stamets' Books:

- Fungi Perfecti
  <http://www.mushroomcompany.com/ >
- The Mushroom Cultivator
  <http://www.amazon.com/The-Mushroom-
  Cultivator-Practical-Mushrooms/dp/0961079800>
- Growing Gourmet and Medicinal Mushrooms
  <http://www.amazon.com/Growing-Gourmet-
  Medicinal-Mushrooms-Stamets/dp/1580081754>

  Also see: Paul Stamets YouTube Channel.
  <http://www.youtube.com/paulstamets>

Field and Forest Products
Home cultivation supplies, kits, spawn, and books.
<http://www.fieldforest.net>

Mushroom Mountain
Bulk spawn, plug spawn, extracts, kits, mycogardening
supplies, workshops.
<http://shop.mushroommountain.com>

Mushroom People
Online catalog of mushroom spawn, books, and growing supplies. "The Farm" is a surviving commune from the 60's. <http://mushroompeople.com/>

<FungusAmongus.com>
Grow at home kits, dried mushrooms for sale

Mushroom Adventures
Grow at home kits and supplies.
<http://www.mushroomadventures.com/>

Unicorn Bags
Autoclavable plastic bags for spawn.
<http://unicornbags.com>

Spore Trading Post
Cultivation Supplies, magic mushroom emphasis
<http://www.sporetradingpost.com/>

Mycosource.com
Fun Guy Farm. Kits, spawn, log inoculation video
<http://www.mycosource.com/>

The Mushroom Patch
The Mushroom Patch. Kits, spawn, spore syringes, spores, books, supplies. <http://www.themushroompatch.com/>

How to Grow Mushrooms at Home

Everything Mushroom
Books, ready to grow mushroom kits, dried wild gourmet mushrooms, outdoor garden patches, mushroom logs, mushroom cultures and spawn, gifts, art
<http://everythingmushrooms.com/>

Mycopath
Mushroom cultivation supplies. Liquid culture syringes available. <http://www.mycopath.com/>

Organja
Mushroom kits, supplies, spores into substrate
<http://organja.com/>

Bioculture
British—Cultures, supplies, cultivation info.
<http://www.bioculture.co.uk/>

Lost Creek Shiitake
Since 1992 sending mushroom log kits to shiitake lovers and gardeners. Shiitake log kits.
<http://www.shiitakemushroomlog.com/>

MycoSupply
Extensive inventory of quality, professional level cultivation supplies: pressure cookers, lab equipment and supplies, glove boxes, transportable grow room, and much more. <http://www.mycosupply.com/>

Wylie Mycologicals
Mycological laboratory, spawn rooms and growing chambers. <http://www.wyliemycologicals.ca/>

Mushroom Shack <http://www.mushroomshack.com/>

Commercial Cultivation

Phillip's Farms
A major commercial supplier of specialty mushrooms. Pennsylvania. <http://www.mushroomshack.com/>

Monterey Mushrooms, Inc
A major commercial supplier of specialty mushrooms. California <http://www.montereymushrooms.com/>

American Mushroom Institute
National voluntary trade association representing the growers, processors, and marketers of cultivated mushrooms in the United States and industry suppliers worldwide. <http://www.americanmushroom.org/>

MushroomCompany.com
Publishes the Mushroom Growers Newsletter. <http://www.mushroomcompany.com/>

Gourmet Mushrooms, Inc.
A major producer of specialty mushrooms. Sebastopol, CA
<http://www.gourmetmushroomsinc.com/>

Canadian Mushroom Growers Association
A voluntary, non-profit organization dedicated to the
production and marketing of fresh mushrooms in Canada.
<http://www.mushrooms.ca/>

Forest Mushrooms <http://www.forestmushrooms.com/>

Modern Mushroom Farms
Suppliers of "whites" (Agaricus bisporus) .
<http://www.modernmush.com/>

MycoLogical Natural Products
<http://www.mycological.com/>

American Mushroom Hunter
<http://www.mushroomhunter.com/>

Manuals and Articles on Mushroom Cultivation

ATTRA Mushroom Cultivation and Marketing
<https://attra.ncat.org/>

"Introduction to Shiitake
<http://www.ca.uky.edu/agc/pubs/for/for78/FOR78.PDF>

How to Grow Mushrooms at Home

Resources for Shiitake
<http://www.ca.uky.edu/agc/pubs/for/for89/for89.pdf>

Training Manual on Mushroom Cultivation Technology
<http://www.unapcaem.org/publication/TM-Mushroom.pdf >

Shiitake Mushroom Production on Logs
<https://store.aces.edu/ItemDetail.aspx?ProductID=15612 >

Six steps to Mushroom Farming .Button mushroom farming. <http://extension.psu.edu/mushroom-grower-info/publications/guides/SixSteps.pdf>

Mushroom Cultivation for People with Disabilities - A Training Manual. An entire manual available in html or pdf a project sponsored by the United Nations Food and Agriculture Organization (FAO) <http://www.fao.org/docrep/004/AB497E/ab497e00.htm>

Six Steps to Mushroom Farming - From Penn State. <http://plantpath.psu.edu/facilities/mushroom/cultures-spawn>

Cultivation of Oyster. An outstanding well-illustrated manual (12 pages) from Penn State. <http://pubs.cas.psu.edu/freepubs/pdfs/UL207.pdf>

How to Grow Mushrooms at Home

Cultivation of Shiitake
<http://pubs.cas.psu.edu/FreePubs/pdfs/xl0083.pdf >

Shiitake and Oyster Mushrooms
<http://www.uky.edu/Ag/NewCrops/introsheets/mushroo ms.pdf>

Cultivating mushrooms in natural logs. Article from The Mushroom People
<http://www.thefarm.org/etc/shiitake.html >

Seasonal Chef Mushroom kit review.
<http://www.seasonalchef.com/mushrooms.htm>

Countryside Magazine Article; Joe Krawczyk interview; Shitake log cultivation.
<http://www.countrysidemag.com/84-5/countryside_staff/>

Oyster Article from Wylie Mycologicals on *Pluerotus* of color
<http://www.wyliemycologicals.ca/Colourful_Mush.pdf>

Growing Shiitake:
<http://extension.missouri.edu/explorepdf/agguides/agrofo restry/af1010.pdf>

Growing Mushrooms with Hydrogen Peroxide
<http://www.mycomasters.com>

Ralf Kurtzman's Oyster
<http://www.oystermushrooms.net>

Mycological Society Sites

Colorado Mycological Society
<http://www.cmsweb.org/articles/cultivation_1.htm>

Kitsap Penninsula Mycological Society
<http://www.dietzfarm.com/growmushrooms>

Sonoma County Mycological Association
<http://www.somamushrooms.org/growing/>

Mykoweb
<http://www.mykoweb.com/articles/cultivation.html>

University Sites

Penn State Mushroom Spawn Laboratory
<http://plantpath.psu.edu/facilities/mushroom/cultures-spawn>

Purdue University specialty mushroom site
<http://www.hort.purdue.edu/newcrop/nexus/mushroom_nex.html>

How to Grow Mushrooms at Home

Cornell University Mushroom Cultivation
<http://blogs.cornell.edu/mushrooms/>

Agricultural Marketing Resource Center (Mushrooms)
<http://www.agmrc.org/commodities_products/specialty_crops/mushrooms_profile.cfm>

Mushroom Recipes

<http://www.fungi.com/blog-archive/tag/Mushroom+Recipes.html>

<http://www.food.com/recipes/mushrooms>

<http://www.huffingtonpost.com/2012/05/07/mushroom-recipes_n_1478550.html>

<http://www.mrfood.com/Editors-Picks/28-Mouthwatering-Mushroom-Recipes#>

<http://www.huffingtonpost.com/2012/05/07/mushroom-recipes_n_1478550.html>

Glossary

A

Abort: A mushroom that stops growing for some reason and never matures.

Acidic: pH lower than 7.

Adnate: Where the gills or tubes beneath the cap of a fungus are at right angles to the stem at the point of attachment

Adnexed: Area of a mushroom where the gills or tubes under the cap sweep upwards before the stem

Aerial mycelium: Hyphal elements that grow above the Agar surface.

Agar: A seaweed extract used to solidify substrate.

Agaric: Mushrooms that have gills under a cap that is connected to a stem.

Alkaline: pH greater than 7.

Annulus: when the tissue ring at the stem of a mushroom ruptures as the fruit develops

Antibiotic: Natural and synthetic compounds that restrain the growth of or eradicate bacteria.

Aseptic: Sterile condition where no undesirable organisms exist.

Autoclave: Pressure cooker that operates at higher pressure than 15 PSI to achieve sterilization temperature (above 250°F.)

B

Bacteria: Microorganisms that can contaminate and also those that are beneficial and required for fruiting of certain species.

Basidiomycetes: Fungi that produce spores externally on basidia.

Birthing: Removing fully colonized growth medium from its container and outing it in circumstances favorable to fruiting.

Bolete: These fungi having tubes instead of gills.

Brown Rice Flour: (BRF) Ground brown rice

Buffer: A system able to oppose changes in pH even when acid or base is added.

C

Calcium Chloride (CaCl2): Drying agent.

Calcium carbonate (CaCO3): A casing ingredient found in limestone.

Cap: The top part of a mushroom.

Carbon Dioxide (CO2): A colorless, odorless, incombustible gas that is created during respiration, combustion, and organic decomposition.

Casing: A covering layer of soil with a particular microflora for fruiting that can be peat, coco coir and vermiculite with limestone and crushed oyster shells.

Cellulose: Glucose polysaccharide that is the main component of plant cell walls.

Cobweb mold: Common name for Dactylium, a mold that is commonly seen on the casing soil or the mushroom that looks like a cobweb.

Colonization: The mushroom cultivation period from Inoculation when the mycelium grows through the substrate until completely permeated.

Compost: The fermented (or fermenting) substrate for growing mushrooms.

Contamination: Undesired foreign contaminants in a substrate or growing medium.

Cottony: Loose and coarse texture.

Culture: Mushroom mycelium growing on a culture medium.

D

Deciduous: Trees and plants that shed their leaves at the end of the growing season.

Desiccant: An anhydrous (waterless) substance, commonly a powder or gel, utilized to absorb water from other substances.

Dextrose (Glucose): A simple sugar utilized in Agar formulations.

Dicaryotic mycelium: Contains the nuclei of both sexes to produce fruiting bodies.

E

Endospore: A metabolically dormant state of bacteria.

Enzyme: A protein synthesized by a cell that works as a catalyst in chemical reaction.

F

Flush: When many mushrooms fruit at the same time typically in a cycle.

Fruiting: When the Mycelium will form mushrooms. Mushrooms are the fruiting bodies of the Mycelium.

Fruiting body: The part of the mushroom that grows above ground.

Fruiting chamber: This is enclosed man made area with high humidity and air exchange for mushroom fruiting.

Fungicide: A class of pesticides used to kill fungi, chiefly those which cause diseases of plants.

Fungus: A group of organisms that decompose organic material, returning nutrients to the soil.

G

Genotype: The set of genes possessed by a single organism.

Germination: Hyphae spreading from a spore.

Gills: The tiny segments on the underside of the cap where the spores come from.

Gypsum: Calcium sulfate, CaSO4. A powder used in spawn making that helps prevent grain clumping and as a pH-buffer.

H

Hygrometer: Instrument that measures relative humidity.

Hypha (e): Filamentous makeup which exhibits apical growth and is the developmental unit of a Mycelium.

I

Incubation: Time period after inoculation when the mycelium grows.

Inoculation: Introduction of spores or spawn into substrate.

L

Lamellae: Mushroom gills.

Lignin: A complex polymer that arises in the woody portion of plants that is highly resistant to chemical and enzymatic degradation.

M

Metabolism: The biochemical processes that maintain a living cell or organism.

Mycelium: The part of the mushroom that grows underneath the ground. This is similar to roots for pants. Mycelium networks can grow very large.

Mycorrhiza: A symbiotic association between a plant root and fungus.

O

Overlay: A thick growth of mycelia that covers the surface of the casing surface; Caused by dry casing, low humidity, or high levels of carbon dioxide.

Oyster shells: Ground and added to casing to achieve a better structure and buffer the pH.

P

Parasitic: Fungi that feed off other living organisms

Pasteurization: Heat applied to a substrate to destroy undesirable organisms while keeping positive ones.

Peat: Unconsolidated soil made up largely of organic matter that has not yet decomposed; used as casing ingredient.

Perlite: Light mineral with millions of microscopic pores that when damp increase humidity.

pH: A measure of the acidity of a medium. pH 7 is neutral; high pH is Alkaline and low pH is Acidic.

Pileus: The mushroom cap.

Pinhead: A young mushroom when the cap is the size of a pin

Primordium: The initial fruiting body stage before forming a pinhead.

R

Rhyzomorph: The appearance of the mycelium of some mushroom strains.

S

Saprophyte: A Fungus that feeds on dead organisms

Selective medium: Medium that allows the growth of certain types of microorganisms.

Spawn: The pure culture of mycelium used to inoculate the final substrate.

Spawn run: The vegetative growth period of the mycelium after spawning.

Spores: The microscopic seeds of mushrooms produced in millions.

Stem: The stalk of a growing mushroom.

Sterilization: The destruction of all micro organisms present by heat or chemicals. Spawn substrate must be sterilize before inoculation.

Stipe: The top part of the stem of a mushroom where the cap is attached.

Strain: Strains vary in genetics but are reproductive compatible.

Stroma: Thick mycelia growth and no fruiting. This condition happens if spawn are exposed to harmful petroleum-based fumes or chemicals or in dry environments.

Substrate: Material used to grow mushrooms. Different mushroom grow better in different substrates such as rye grain, straw, rice, compost, woodchips, and so on. birdseed).

T

Tissue culture: Tissue cultures are a sample of a mushroom or mycelia. Cultures are obtained by removing a piece of the mushroom cap or stem in sterile conditions and placing the sample on an agar plate. Mycelium grows from the tissue and colonizes the agar.

Veil: Edges of the mushroom cap break away from the stem during growth leaving a thin veil of material hanging from the stem.

Vermiculite: Highly absorbent material made from puffed mica that helps hold water when used in rice cakes.

Z

Zonate: Marked with concentric bands of color such as the appearance of mycelium of some mushroom species.

Index

16648075R00074

Made in the USA
Middletown, DE
18 December 2014